INVENTIONS THAT CHANGED THE WORLD
VACCINES

BY SARA GREEN

Bellwether Media • Minneapolis, MN

Blastoff! Discovery launches a new mission: reading to learn. Filled with facts and features, each book offers you an exciting new world to explore!

This edition first published in 2022 by Bellwether Media, Inc.

No part of this publication may be reproduced in whole or in part without written permission of the publisher.
For information regarding permission, write to Bellwether Media, Inc.,
Attention: Permissions Department,
6012 Blue Circle Drive, Minnetonka, MN 55343.

Library of Congress Cataloging-in-Publication Data

Names: Green, Sara, 1964- author.
Title: Vaccines / by Sara Green.
Description: Minneapolis, MN : Bellwether Media, 2022. | Series: Inventions that changed the world | Includes bibliographical references and index. | Audience: Ages 7-13 | Audience: Grades 4-6 | Summary: "Engaging images accompany information about vaccines. The combination of high-interest subject matter and narrative text is intended for students in grades 3 through 8"– Provided by publisher.
Identifiers: LCCN 2021049230 (print) | LCCN 2021049231 (ebook) | ISBN 9781644876183 (library binding) | ISBN 9781648346811 (paperback) | ISBN 9781648346293 (ebook)
Subjects: LCSH: Vaccines–Juvenile literature. | Vaccination–Juvenile literature.
Classification: LCC RA638 .G74 2022 (print) | LCC RA638 (ebook) | DDC 615.3/72–dc23/eng/20211007
LC record available at https://lccn.loc.gov/2021049230
LC ebook record available at https://lccn.loc.gov/2021049231

Text copyright © 2022 by Bellwether Media, Inc. BLASTOFF! DISCOVERY and associated logos are trademarks and/or registered trademarks of Bellwether Media, Inc.

Editor: Rebecca Sabelko   Designer: Josh Brink

Printed in the United States of America, North Mankato, MN.

TABLE OF CONTENTS

ON SAFARI! 4

EARLY LIFESAVERS 8

BOOSTING THE IMMUNE SYSTEM 18

BUILDING PROTECTION 22

VACCINE UPGRADES 26

VACCINE TIMELINE 28

GLOSSARY 30

TO LEARN MORE 31

INDEX 32

ON SAFARI!

A family is going on safari in Africa! The travel company sends information about the vaccines the family needs to get. These vaccines will help everyone stay healthy during their trip.

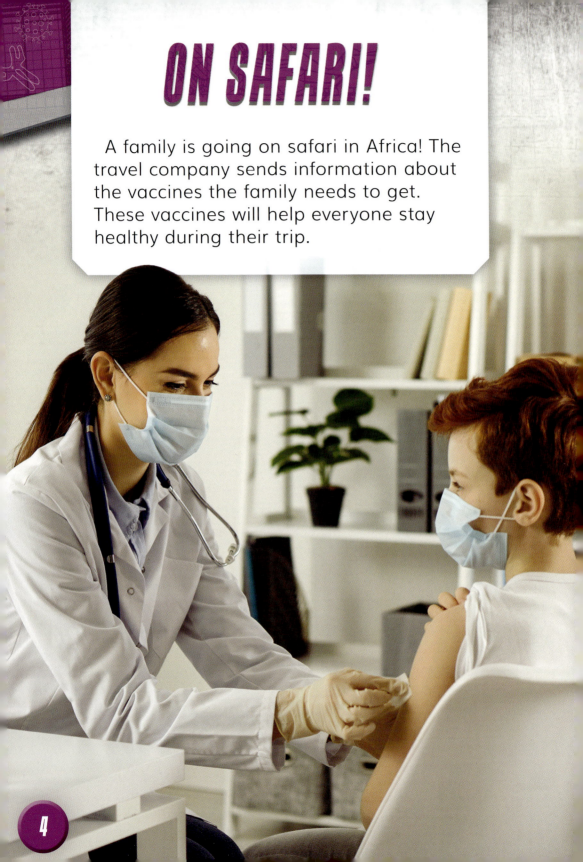

Some family members are nervous to get shots. The doctor makes the visit easy. First, she checks that everyone's vaccinations are up to date. Then, she gives each person the two shots needed for the trip. The **injections** feel like little pinches. Soon, they are done!

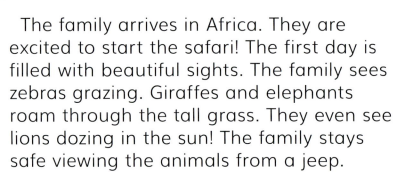

The family arrives in Africa. They are excited to start the safari! The first day is filled with beautiful sights. The family sees zebras grazing. Giraffes and elephants roam through the tall grass. They even see lions dozing in the sun! The family stays safe viewing the animals from a jeep.

The family also stays safe from dangerous germs. With vaccines, everyone can enjoy the safari in good health!

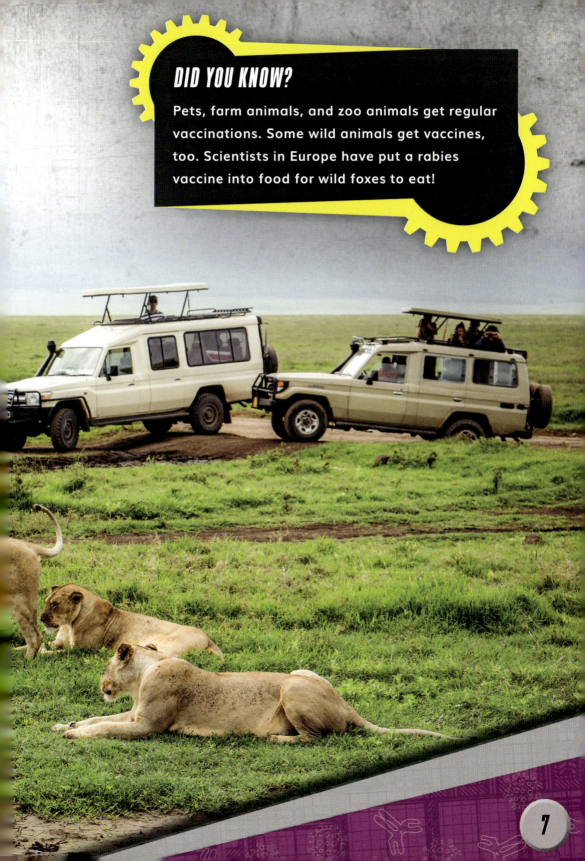

DID YOU KNOW?

Pets, farm animals, and zoo animals get regular vaccinations. Some wild animals get vaccines, too. Scientists in Europe have put a rabies vaccine into food for wild foxes to eat!

EARLY LIFESAVERS

Vaccines help the body prevent diseases caused by harmful germs. They work with the body's **immune system** to fight **viruses** and **bacteria**.

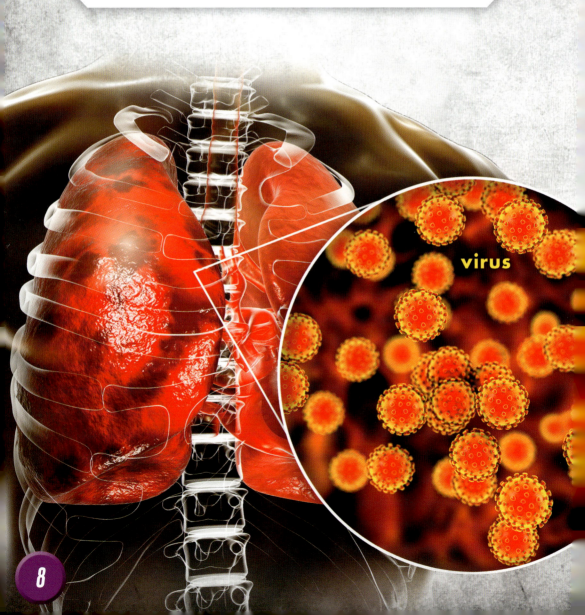

virus

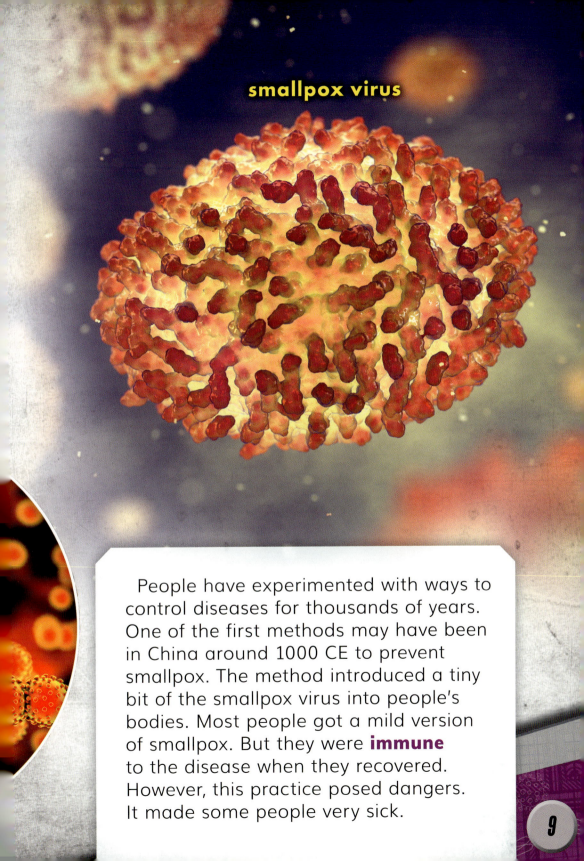

smallpox virus

People have experimented with ways to control diseases for thousands of years. One of the first methods may have been in China around 1000 CE to prevent smallpox. The method introduced a tiny bit of the smallpox virus into people's bodies. Most people got a mild version of smallpox. But they were **immune** to the disease when they recovered. However, this practice posed dangers. It made some people very sick.

Edward Jenner discovered a safer way to protect people against smallpox in the 1790s.

Edward Jenner

DID YOU KNOW?

There are only two known smallpox samples left in the world. They are held in labs. They have higher security than a nuclear bomb!

Jenner learned that dairy workers who got a mild disease called cowpox did not get smallpox. This gave him the idea to **inoculate** people with the cowpox germ. The vaccination kept people safe from smallpox. It was a huge success. The disease was officially destroyed worldwide in 1980.

In the 1800s, a French chemist named Louis Pasteur discovered how to make vaccines from weakened germs. He developed several vaccines. One was the first rabies vaccine.

Louis Pasteur

Louis Pasteur's lab equipment

More vaccines were developed during the early 1900s. They included diphtheria, tetanus, and whooping cough. These deadly diseases were once common in both children and adults. Vaccines greatly lowered their infection rates. In 1948, the three vaccines were combined into the DTP vaccine. One shot protected people against three diseases!

PIONEER PROFILE

JONAS SALK

Born: October 28, 1914, in New York City, New York
Died: June 23, 1995
Background: Jonas Salk was an American doctor and medical scientist
Vaccine Invented: Polio
Year Released: 1955
Idea Development: Salk discovered that the dead polio virus protected monkeys from getting the disease. He created a polio vaccine from the dead virus. He tested it on many people. He even tested it on himself. The vaccine was both safe and effective!

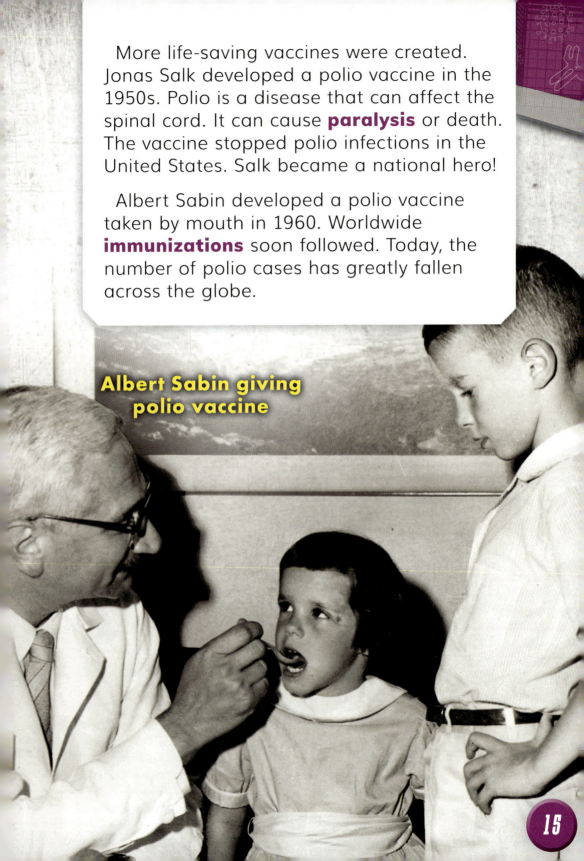

More life-saving vaccines were created. Jonas Salk developed a polio vaccine in the 1950s. Polio is a disease that can affect the spinal cord. It can cause **paralysis** or death. The vaccine stopped polio infections in the United States. Salk became a national hero!

Albert Sabin developed a polio vaccine taken by mouth in 1960. Worldwide **immunizations** soon followed. Today, the number of polio cases has greatly fallen across the globe.

Albert Sabin giving polio vaccine

The 1960s saw the development of vaccines for measles, mumps, and rubella. These diseases infected millions of people in the U.S. every year. Nearly all children got measles by the time they were 15 years old. Today, these diseases are rare in the U.S.

New vaccines are still made today. Scientists rushed to develop safe vaccines when the COVID-19 **pandemic** started in 2019. Success came within 12 months. The COVID-19 vaccines were made in record time!

COVID-19 vaccine production

VACCINES PROFILE

COVID-19 mRNA VACCINES

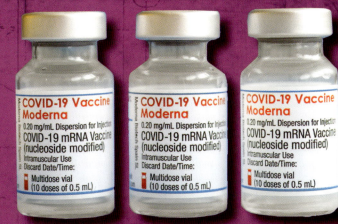

Inventors' Names: Scientists Katalin Karikó and Drew Weissman discovered how to use mRNA to make effective vaccines.

Year of Release: 2020

How the Vaccines Are Used: The COVID-19 mRNA vaccines teach cells how to make a piece of the virus. The immune system learns what the bad germs look like and destroys them.

DID YOU KNOW?

Two of the COVID-19 vaccines are mRNA vaccines. They are the first mRNA vaccines with widespread human use!

BOOSTING THE IMMUNE SYSTEM

Vaccines work in different ways. The vaccine for measles, mumps, and rubella contains little pieces of germs. The germs are either weak or dead and harmless. Other vaccines introduce a tiny amount of **toxin** into the body.

The immune system detects the weakened germs or toxins. Then, it begins making **antibodies** to destroy them. Information about the germs is stored in **memory cells**. The cells recognize harmful versions of the germs if they enter the body. They quickly attack!

HOW IT WORKS

VACCINES

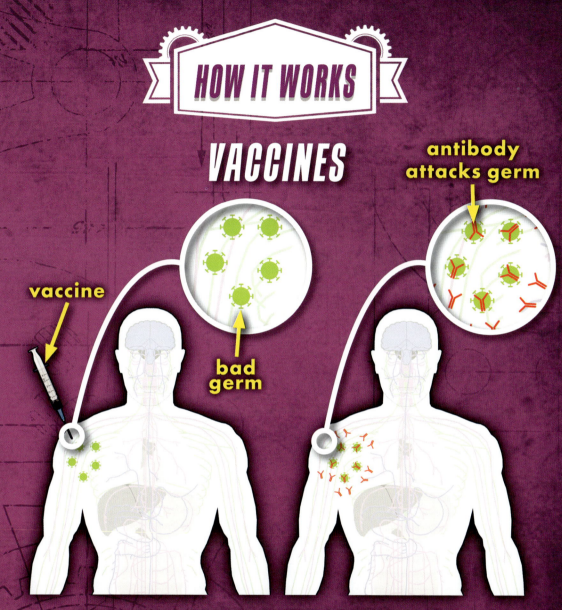

- People are given a vaccine that has a small amount of a harmless form of a bad germ.

- The immune system makes antibodies. They attack and destroy the germ.

- The immune system remembers the germ. It will attack the real germs if they invade the body later.

Most vaccines are injected into the body with needles. A doctor or nurse injects the vaccine into a muscle.

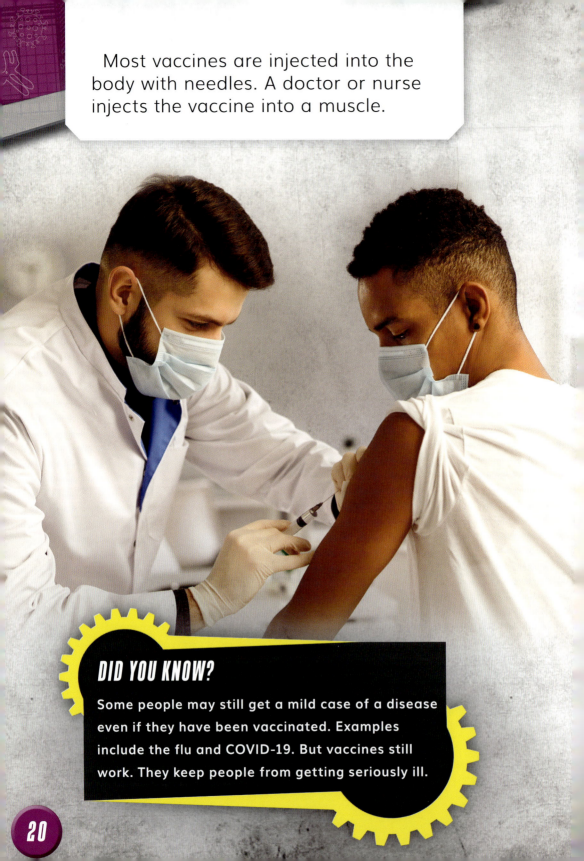

DID YOU KNOW?

Some people may still get a mild case of a disease even if they have been vaccinated. Examples include the flu and COVID-19. But vaccines still work. They keep people from getting seriously ill.

baby getting rotavirus vaccine

Vaccines also come in other forms. Flu vaccines come as both shots and sprays given in the nose. **Jet injectors** can also be used to give vaccines. They use pressure to push liquid into the skin. Some vaccines come as liquid drops put into the mouth. Babies get the rotavirus vaccine this way.

BUILDING PROTECTION

Vaccines continue to protect people from serious diseases. Most vaccines are given during childhood. They cover around 14 different diseases. Many adults also get vaccines. They include the seasonal flu vaccine and the shingles vaccine. Some vaccines need **boosters**. The tetanus vaccine is needed every 10 years.

people waiting to get COVID-19 vaccine

Vaccines can protect communities through **herd immunity**. This happens when most people in a community are vaccinated against a disease. Germs cannot easily spread from person to person. Herd immunity is especially important for people who cannot get certain vaccines.

23

Vaccines prevent millions of deaths around the world every year. But people still die from diseases that vaccines could prevent. Many of them live in remote areas or where there is war. It can be difficult to get vaccines to people in these areas.

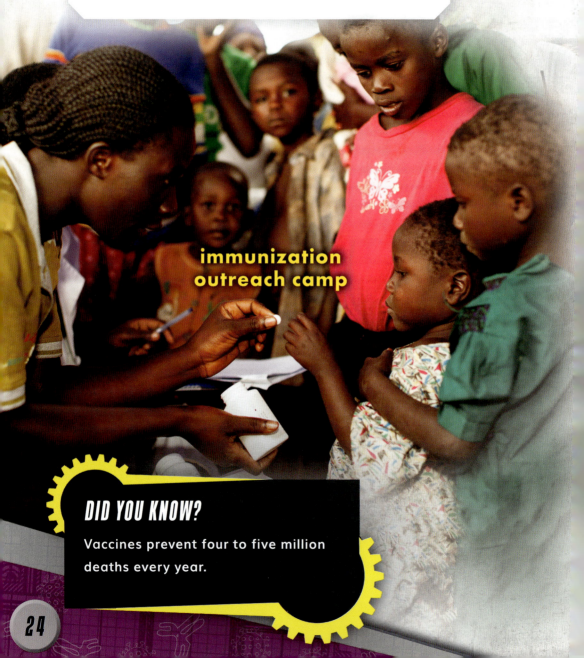

immunization outreach camp

DID YOU KNOW?

Vaccines prevent four to five million deaths every year.

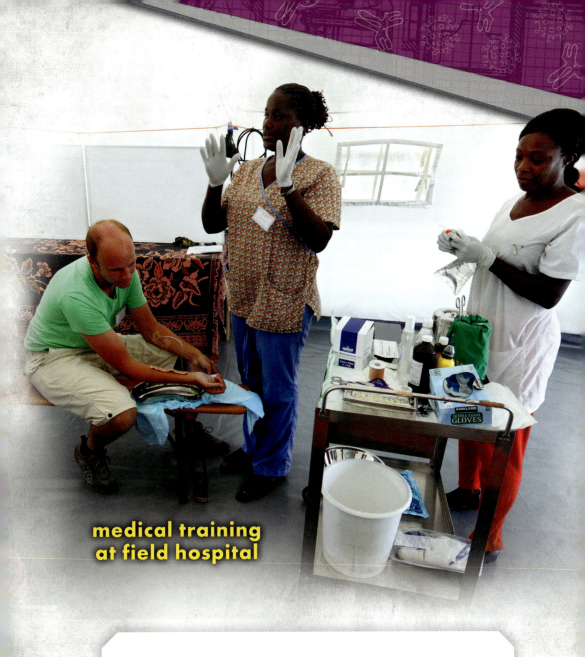

medical training at field hospital

Relief organizations around the world are working to solve this problem. They give information about vaccinations to people. They also provide training and **PPE** to health care workers. The world is getting closer to freedom from many deadly diseases with their help.

VACCINE UPGRADES

Vaccine technology continues to advance. Scientists are developing painless vaccines called **microneedle patches**. They stick to the skin. The patches are easy to transport and store. They could help boost vaccination programs around the world!

enlarged model of a microneedle patch

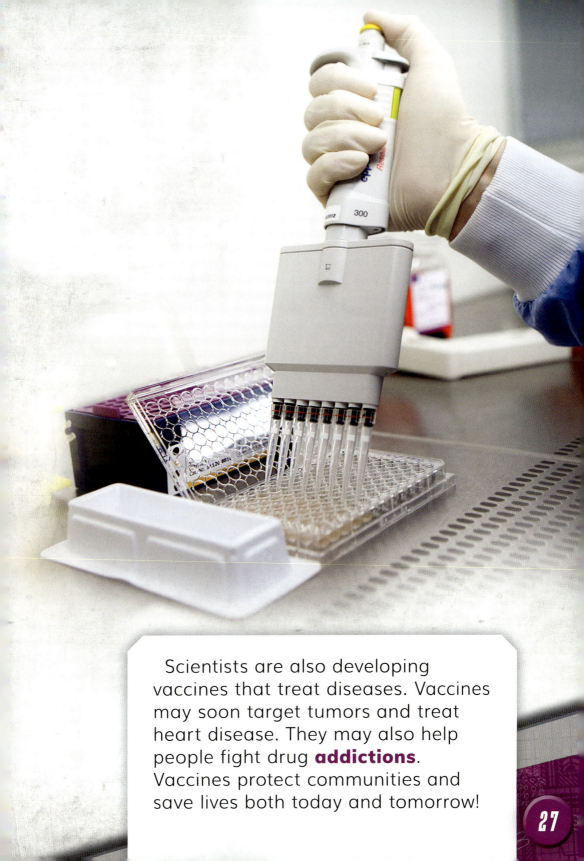

  Scientists are also developing vaccines that treat diseases. Vaccines may soon target tumors and treat heart disease. They may also help people fight drug **addictions**. Vaccines protect communities and save lives both today and tomorrow!

VACCINE TIMELINE

1796

Edward Jenner develops the first smallpox vaccine

1945

The first flu vaccine is approved

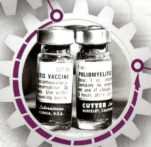

1885

Louis Pasteur develops the first rabies vaccine

1955

The first polio vaccine is available in the U.S.

1991
Polio is ended in the Western Hemisphere

2020
The first mRNA vaccines are approved for use against COVID-19

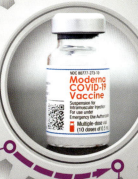

2022-
Future developments

2021
Almost half of the world's population has received a dose of a COVID-19 vaccine

1980
The World Health Assembly states that the world is free of naturally-occuring smallpox

29

GLOSSARY

addictions—great needs to do or have something

antibodies—proteins made by the body's immune system when it detects harmful substances

bacteria—single-celled living things that usually live in soil, water, or in plants and animals; bacteria can cause diseases.

boosters—extra doses of a vaccine given over time to strengthen the immune system

herd immunity—protection from a disease that is only possible when many people in a community are immune to the disease

immune—not capable of being infected by a disease

immune system—the system in the body that helps protect against diseases

immunizations—treatments to create immunities to diseases

injections—the act of forcing liquid medicines or vaccines into the body using a special needle

inoculate—to inject a very small amount of a disease to help resist that disease in the future

jet injectors—devices that use high pressure to push fluid beneath the skin

memory cells—cells that remember invaders that have already attacked the body; cells are the smallest parts of living things.

microneedle patches—small patches that have hundreds of tiny needles clustered together to deliver medicine or vaccines

pandemic—an outbreak of a disease that happens over a wide area and affects many people

paralysis—the loss of the ability to move

PPE—personal protective equipment; PPE is special clothing or equipment used to prevent contact with dangerous substances.

toxin—a poison made by a living thing

viruses—tiny germs that can infect people, animals, and plants and make them sick

TO LEARN MORE

AT THE LIBRARY

Denton, Michelle. *Pandemics: Deadly Disease Outbreaks*. New York, N.Y.: Lucent Press, 2020.

Jenner, Elizabeth, Kate Wilson, and Nia Roberts. *Coronavirus: A Book for Children*. Somerville, Mass.: Candlewick Press, 2020.

Levine, Sara. *Germs Up Close*. Minneapolis, Minn.: Millbrook Press, 2021.

ON THE WEB

FACTSURFER

Factsurfer.com gives you a safe, fun way to find more information.

1. Go to www.factsurfer.com.

2. Enter "vaccines" into the search box and click 🔍.

3. Select your book cover to see a list of related content.

INDEX

addictions, 27

Africa, 4, 6

antibodies, 18

bacteria, 8

boosters, 22

China, 9

COVID-19, 16, 17, 20, 23

cowpox, 11

diphtheria, 13

DTP, 13

flu, 20, 21, 22

heart disease, 27

herd immunity, 23

how it works, 19

immune, 9

immune system, 8, 18

immunizations, 15

injections, 5, 20

Jenner, Edward, 10, 11

jet injectors, 21

measles, 16, 18

memory cells, 18

microneedle patches, 26

mRNA vaccines, 17

mumps, 16, 18

Pasteur, Louis, 12, 13

polio, 15

PPE, 25

prevention, 24

rabies, 7, 12

rotavirus, 21

rubella, 16, 18

Sabin, Albert, 15

Salk, Jonas, 14, 15

shingles, 22

shots, 5, 13, 21

smallpox, 9, 10, 11

sprays, 21

tetanus, 13, 22

timeline, 28–29

toxin, 18

tumors, 27

United States, 15, 16

viruses, 8, 9

whooping cough, 13

The images in this book are reproduced through the courtesy of: Miguel Toro, front cover (Moderna & AstraZeneca); mundissima, front cover (Pfizer); Grook Da Oger/ Wiki Commons, front cover (H1N1); Whispyhistory/ Wiki Commons, front cover; Arkadi Bulva, front cover (medical syringe); Svetsol, front cover (virus); Krzepax, front cover (antibodies); Studio Romantic, pp. 4-5, 20; Kanokratnok, pp. 6-7; Kateryna Kon, p. 8; nobeastsofierce, p. 9; The History Collection/ Alamy, p. 10; Photo Researchers/ Alamy, p. 11; Lanmas/ Alamy, p. 12; Photo 12/ Alamy, p. 13; RBM Vintage Images, p. 14; Photo12/Ann Ronan Picture Library/ Alamy, p. 15; Artyom Geodakyan/ Getty Images, p. 16; Marcos del Maz/ Alamy, p. 17; Lightspring, p. 18; Phanie/ Alamy, p. 21; Sofia Shunkina/ Alamy, p. 22; Operation 2021/ Alamy, p. 23; Jake Lyell/ Alamy, p. 24; Agencja Fotograficzna Caro/ Alamy, p. 25; MediaNews Group/ Reading Eagle via Getty Images/ Getty Images, p. 26; BSIP/ Getty Images, p. 27; National Portrait Library/ Wiki Commons, p. 28 (Edward Jenner); Harvard Art Museum/Fogg Museum/ Wiki Commons, p. 28 (Louis Pasteur); Interim Archives/ Getty Images, p. 28 (first flu vaccine); New York Daily News Archive/ Getty Images, p. 28 (first polio vaccine); Smith Collection/Gado/ Getty Images, p. 29 (World Health Assembly); Bob London/ Alamy, p. 29 (polio vaccine); Governor Tom Wolf/ Wiki Commons, p. 29 (mRNA); Prostock-studio, p. 29 (vaccination); Gorodenkoff, p. 29 (future).